Lover's Life Past

Samantha Friello

iUniverse, Inc.
Bloomington

Lover's Life Past

iUniverse books may be ordered through booksellers or by contacting:

iUniverse
1663 Liberty Drive
Bloomington, IN 47403
www.iuniverse.com
1-800-Authors (1-800-288-4677)

ISBN: 978-1-4620-2030-0 (sc)
ISBN: 978-1-4620-2031-7 (e)

Printed in the United States of America

iUniverse rev. date: 05/18/2011

CONTENTS

TO STEAL HIM BACK AGAIN

making a lasting impression
on the object of your affection
salivating and drooling
over him
a minor imperfection
striking attributes
which stand to condone
shooting daggers at her
while turning her into stone

the time has come
for you to
roll up your sleeves
willing to believe
that you can actually
steal him back again
and then leave
his languid gait
and mesmerizing smile
melting your insides
as you decide
to stay for awhile

a playful game
of cat and mouse
is all that you seek
for you will
always remember
how she swept him
off his feet
all efforts will remain
dire and futile
until you figure out
a way for him to
unregrettably lose her

acknowledging the fact
that you will inevitably win
for you have committed
the most heinous of sins
quenching your thirst
for smooth flesh and skin
by stealing him back again
the way you did back then

PINK EYE

grinding your fists
into your eyes
trying to alleviate
a burning itch
which won't subside
bleeding capillaries
and veins
turning the whites
of your eyes gray
sneezing into soft tissue
after having coughed
and heaved
another prevailing issue

too late to realize
that damage
has been done
a run-down body
ignoring the fact
that the time has come
administering
various creams
and eye drops
promising to
guarantee instant relief
an incorrect diagnosis
and an eyesore
hindering your ability
to see

a glimmer of light
and a degree
of finesse needed
to calm yourself down
for you have waited
seven days
for bleeding red
to plummet
and then drown

intently watching
your right eye
become clearer
rehashing
what it was
that has brought
you here

stress becoming
much worse
than it was before
a derogatory choice
of words
erasing every care
in the world
rising degrees
and a sweltering heat
making you forget
the person
whom you have agreed
to meet

your eyeball
slowly healing
without a trace of infection
or vehement sore
smoky gray and a
vast array of essentials
displaying eyes
which will never forgo
an opportunity
to show off
a spiteful distraction
for those who continue
to gape in awe
at a superficial
and short-lived flaw

INNER COMPASS

dazzling diamonds
and precious jewels
sparkling only
when you wanted them to
a skimpy costume
of black leather and lace
long, silk scarves
barely leaving a trace
scorching, red marks
traveling up your spine
a rug burn disappearing
in just a moment's time
a performance sworn
to uplift his mood
acting out
various characters
just to keep him fooled
becoming extinct
is your guilty conscience
as you continuously try
to reset your inner compass

A PERMANENT FIXTURE

a round, furry ball
sulking in your lap
a slow, steady purr
coming from her long,
winter's nap
a comforting night spent
by the fire
as you roll out
your blanket for her
laying beside your cat's
soft, luxurious fur

black and white spots
marking her coat
as you kneel down
to pet her as she mopes
her silent, brooding eyes
shining bittersweet joy
for she is more than happy
to be a permanent fixture
along with her brand-new toy

having had enough to eat
for she has chowed down
until her bowl is licked clean
a reminder of when
you were small
taking care of everything
she has foretold
your blessed, little angel
designating a sacred place
for you in her heart
intuitively knowing
when you will have to spend
the day apart

climbing upon your bed
as you toss and turn at night
for she is the one born
with bewitching,
nocturnal sight
a sweet, innocent face
making your heart ache
as vibrant, glowing eyes
lead a pathway
to your side

a sweet, morning kiss
feeling her
walking all over you
at her own risk
happily licking your face
as you contemplate a way
to make her go away
awakening from
a deep slumber
as she meows
at phantom beings
she can only see
clawing at sheer,
summer curtains
continuing to sway
in the breeze

flying bugs and a whimper
foretelling when someone
will utter a slight whisper
a sanctuary for the rest
of her feline friends
as she stares
out the door at them
acknowledging her gratitude
and thanks
as she places her paws
upon your shanks

A NUTRITIONAL DEFICIT

a calm and exquisite peace
stealing over you
as you drop your bags
to chew on cracked corn
and sunflower seeds
sale racks full of fruity gum,
delectable chocolate bars,
and Caribbean rum

graham crackers
crumbling in your grasp
as you lay down
dollar bills, candy wrappers,
and trash
a misty and rainy afternoon
turning into an evening
with nothing else to do
but sit down and chew
on treats
reserved just for you

a frivolous commodity
drowning out deafening noises
of everyday, miniscule choices
trivial matters on your mind
as you get up to
lower the blinds
for you should have
fallen asleep by now
because it was past
your bedtime

after receiving
a sloppy, goodnight kiss
from your dog
you head back into
a bed chamber once
renovated and then ignored
laying on your side
you stare open-eyed
at your TV
denying yourself
much needed rest and relief

your mind jammed
and preoccupied
for you have forgotten
numerous ingredients
required to concoct
buttery bread, fluffy eggs,
and biscuits
the qualm of necessity
overcoming you
as you reach for
a box of cereal
bran flakes which lack
their essential vitamins
and minerals

WRITER'S BLOCK

trying to force it out of you
disgruntled words
which refuse to let go
scribbled and afraid
to be erased
a minute to assess
what they are trying to say
a forthrightness
and a presupposition to disobey
unleashing jumbled paragraphs
into a crinkled, blank essay
abbreviations and exclamation points
needed to hide your irritation
as you analyze exactly what
catching words should portray
a deep, transformative meditation
uncovering the mysteries of today
a foreign language
dissected from a long ago,
slang interpretation
a hesitant pronunciation
forcing you to investigate
an alternative form
of communication
a style of penmanship
constituting sharp angles
and smooth contours
the apparent misuse
of numerous commas
and semi-colons

DRESSING IN DRAG

a makeup palette
bursting exuberant
splashes of color
dressing in drag
without having to button
a stifling, shirt collar
shoulder-length hair
teased and tamed
for a wig is necessary
to cover the receding hairline
of a notorious dame
a corset reserved
for a night of fun
tying up loose ends
while inhaling air
into constricting lungs
sparkling glitter
embellishing his leather outfit
a made-up face
portraying a texture
of smooth velvet
lipstick placed
upon dry, cracked lips
sipping herbal tea
as a deep, rose blush
stains chiseled cheeks
tweezing out fine, thin hair
intent on shaving
muscular legs
already smooth and bare
an itchy stubble
scratched with long,
manicured fingernails
a beauty regime concluded
by fastening silk stockings
to a lace, garter belt

PROMISE RING

gazing at sparkling jewels
comprising a tentative,
rainbow hue
a blinding light
pushing you onwards
until you come face to face
with a reality
you have pondered
striding purposefully
in all your blazing beauty
as you scope out
deep, display cases
full of expensive,
priceless jewelry

a ricochet effect
as colors collide
a kaleidoscope
of deep, intense reflection
mirroring pastel pinks
and blues
rings so ostentatious
that you cannot choose
gazing longingly at a
simple, elegant ring
until you become blind
from its shattering,
piercing light

never in a hurry
to set a date
for he is acclimated
to the sweet and tender
side of things
heeding all your wishes
while being on call
to wash dirty dishes
a meat and potatoes
kind of man

who only waits for you
to choose between
a thick, juicy steak
or sweet, salty ham

visiting your favorite store
as you daydream of
the night before
repeating the mantra
that you want a ring
bigger and brighter
than any diamond can be
on high alert
from a caffeine rush
as you decide
which style and price
would be too much

rummaging in your wallet
for your cell phone
to call your man
who is to be reprimanded
once again
picking and choosing
whatever it is
that you demand
self-absorbed and unaware
as he holds
your promise ring
in his hand

THE BRUNT OF ALL JOKES

creased, ironed cuffs
and a starched, white shirt
rings of dirt hidden
underneath all the hurt
toting a heavy basket
on broad shoulders
as the potent aroma
of laundry detergent
becomes considerably stronger

taking the time to
button up wrinkled jeans
turning shirts inside out
to get them clean
a day full of chores
making you want to scream
as you patiently wait
for the next, unoccupied,
washing machine

an afternoon
at the Laundromat
is never anything
to laugh at
continuing to pace
up and down
dirty, tile floors
echoing distant laughter
and faint-hearted snores

ready to start
as you jam clothing
into enormous, silver jars
quarters and dimes
toppling alongside
your unwashed bras
trying to force-feed coins
into change dispensers
as you become
the brunt of all jokes
encouraging lively banter

IMAGINARY FRIEND

a slow thaw
and a light dusting
of snow
nesting in
a shallow hole
her feet tingling
with the essence
of a winter storm
making a wise choice
as she bundles up
and traverses
great terrains
all alone
stumbling upon
dirt and rigid stone
pent-up feelings
revealing a heart
which can never heal
twinkling stars
mapping out
a solitary maze
leading her away
from a broad,
muscular frame
a timeless love
centered around
he who has appeared
from up above
a man on the mend
tall, built, and tan
trekking across
desolate land
as her journey ends

LACTOSE TOLERANCE

a whopping scoop
of vanilla cream
mixed in with
rainbow sprinkles
a sugary shell of a cone
cracking into pieces
baking at a high temperature
is a sweltering sun in June
as you quickly consume
an exorbitant amount
of melting, ice cream
with a small, plastic spoon

PEEK A BOO

burrowing deep within
thick comforters and sheets
waiting for dawn and dusk
to finally meet
a seedy, hotel room
challenging her
with another passing whim
a perfect scenario
highlighting
a tall glass of gin
parading around
in fuzzy, red slippers
as she stares into
tall, bathroom mirrors
sharp scissors used
to snip overgrown bangs
windblown hair
becoming tangled
after the sweet song
he sang
sparkling earrings
softly grazing a bosom
enhanced with
rubber inserts,
store-bought cleavage,
and a plastic rebirth
thick hands groping
handfuls of jelly
wiggling and wobbling
while overlapping
a protruding belly
pulling back his hand
after she slaps his cheek
never asking him why
he wanted to peek

NO FRILLS

shamefaced
as the bathroom door
creaks open
admitting a
statuesque frame
of a man
a tall mountain
of numerous misgivings
and a worthless sham

wondering how
you got to be here
a running faucet
gurgling and fizzing
along with a broken toilet
continuously flushing
and wheezing

hot water and a
forceful collision
of wills
leaning against
towel racks
decorated with
intricate lace
and no-nonsense frills

rough, calloused hands
tracing a pathway
along your skin
without a single word
or reprimand
a strong urge to flee
sifting through
flyaway hair
as you stand
as stiff as a tree

roll-on antiperspirant
leaving its mark
as bottles and sprays
inhabit an
ancient washstand
and moveable cart
a transparent, shower curtain
responding with a
muted, peaceful allure
as a rush of water
drowns out
the sullen and the obscure

subtle, colorful stripes
and miniscule, pin-dots
saving countertops
from a dull finish
updating the attributes
of a used washroom
as he installs a brand-new,
sparkling spigot

CAT FIGHT

here is an opportunity
to make him cringe
a foolhardy attempt
as you place your hands
all over him
a fight for territory
as you grab her hair
unable to resist
a mischievous
and instigating dare
maddeningly pulling out
large tufts of amber light
golden streaks
adding a vibrant luster
to a cold and rainy night
casting her out
with a succession
of demeaning words
a courageous state of affairs
and a low blow
shattering her self-worth
provocative clothing
never to be seen in
ripped to shreds
by her sharp claws
as you wept
a bleeding heart
which will never
win you
a golden star
bigger and braver
than what was
expected of her so far
falling from grace
as you hesitantly begin
a catfight
acting out of character
all because of him

KNOWN AS MAN

falling to
the wayside
are feelings
beginning to
subside
a constant battle
between shaky,
self-confidence
and the urgent need
to cry
the abandonment
of his hands
and the inability
to withstand
a deep superficiality
hidden beneath
a gruff exterior
known as man
a shallowness
which can never
be ignored
chiseled stone
and the severe cut
of his bones
unfeeling and cold
as you wrap
your arms around
a disaster
yet to be known

NIGHTY-NITE

blowing off steam
as you slowly
come to terms with
an enraged, jealous being
tender, aching limbs
wearing thin
as you peer through
sheer, summer curtains
choosing to hibernate
with your cat
a ball of fur
contentedly purring
sliding into bed all alone
while scrutinizing
tentative rays
glowing in your home
an illuminating lamplight
casting shadows
upon bare walls
a harsh glare
making your eyes sting
for just a moment more
turning the light off
as you sit in the dark
lost in thought
contemplating a
variety of ways
you could have stated
your case
never taking the time
to listen with an open mind
repulsive images which are
replaced by a variety
of frightful dreams,
omens, and signs
pulling you out
into raging seas
tossing and turning
within tangled folds

of cotton sheets
a long, lean body
interrupting your
droning snores
as you groggily mutter
nighty-nite
to the one you have
chosen to ignore

AT GREAT LENGTH

pulling a brush through
long streaks of color
a spiral perm purchased on
a very tight budget
curls and waves
invading the perfect face
lightening your hair
with each strand in place
going to great lengths
to create the perfect up do
a round brush
dictating what is
in style and cool
a hairnet and gloves
needed to conduct
the infusion
of permanent color
a strand test
incorporating ills
you have just discovered
turning grey at the temples
as you pray for time
to halt and stumble
a fierce determination
attaching itself
to stiff hairspray
as white globs of mousse
make headway
through tresses
which beg you to review
hair scunchies
gathering unruly hair
into an ostentatious do'
succumbing to a
harsh and volatile test
as you quickly grasp
sharp scissors
to cut off the rest

MRS. HIGH AND MIGHTY

designer, stiletto heels
clicking and clacking
on hard-wood floors
decidedly ignoring
a mounting intuition
hovering
as you coincidently
stumble and fall

mumbling beneath
your breath
as you delicately expunge
secrets you have kept
finally acknowledging
the truth
as the telltale signs
of a manic man
divulge you of your
blatant sins
and long-term plans

bursting out of his shell
is a fiery ball of fire
a linear vision
transforming into
a robust and
bloodsucking vampire
disgust kept in tow
as he fervently tries
to swallow you whole
a magnetic force
pulling you away
as he bursts
into a raging flame

restless timbers
smoldering
as you step out
without him knowing
beady eyes
secretly peering
at your expensive,
designer clothes
sparkling diamonds
and earrings
which vibrantly flash
the answer, "no"

a bitter ending to
a dire situation
an outpouring of words
leaving you feeling
bereft and cold
carelessly tossing out
his soiled, tighty-whities
a life-altering choice
decided by
Mrs. High and Mighty

ZEST AND ZEAL

enriched, long grain rice
and a table set for two
long-limbed candlesticks
adding a hint of color
for you
a whimsical setting
boasting a high-rise,
floral arrangement
a pair of winged-back chairs,
embroidered napkins,
and lace tablecloths
to spare

buttered rolls
and a savvy dip to smear
adding a zest and zeal
to a concoction
which will soon appear
brazen, red peppers
and Italian, green olives
an herbal remedy foreseen
as lasting just a little while

peeling layers of onions
into a happening, stir fry
as you ache for someone
to drive by
leaving the windows wide open
to beseech and then deny
a heavenly smell correlated
in order to promote
fanciful dishes of pride

a salad dressing
awaiting a spoon
to dip into
flaky croutons
caking and sticking
to the other side of noon
chunks of mayonnaise
and blended, green vegetables
slowly leaking
onto your favorite shoes

a final entrée
soon to appear
as you disappear
to bring back
love letters you hold dear
thirsty for the sweet taste
of Mountain Dew
as avocados and carrots
add mystery
to a boiling, beef stew

OUT OF THE CLOSET

hanging alongside
fashionable belts
are vintage coats
entailing sequins
and makeshift bows
thinking of those
who will get a
delightful thrill
from the passed-on goods
of a once-idolized girl
spoiled by
a brilliant life
filled with glamorous,
long nights
fleeting memories
of years gone by
helping you extricate
lace delicates
from underneath his eyes
thrifty items meant for
those who can use them
a passing inconvenience
reconsidered
for you will fill up
garbage bags
set aside for another
relentless season
used-up tissues
crinkled and ripped
shoved within deep pockets
of your newest gift
a cashmere sweater
expecting lavish praise
as you pick up a silk blouse
which has seen better days

THE ONLY CONSTANT

tentative steps taken
as I create him
embarking upon
a glorious ride
into the radiant divine
a newer man
whose hazel eyes
are locked within mine
a foolhardy attempt
as I crave
his sweet sentiment
smooth crevices
leaping up to meet him
turning into the
perfect, summer fling
for I can never leave him
coming to an end
is the search
for a perfect love
for he is as surprised
as the stars twinkling
from up above
a sparkling twilight
rotating above us
as a poignant declaration
spills from his mouth
kneeling down
on one knee
as I cry joyfully
unable to comprehend
the reasons why
he has appeared
before me

the only constant
in my life

MAKE NO MISTAKE

make no mistake
about it
for you have never
felt so ecstatic
dusting off layers
of dirt and grime
dreary curtains
which resist the
passage of time
antique, picture frames
rehashing long-ago days
a profound realization
encouraging memories
to be replayed
collecting cleaning supplies
as you attack
one chore at a time
uneven streaks
occupying your wooden blinds
ancient stains on your couch
adding a touch of disdain
to your quizzical brow
perplexed as you
take a look around
at a room which has
never looked as clean
as it does now

WINK

a flirtatious remark
and a snide comment
reading in-between the lines
as your heart plummets
following days which turn
ignorant and mean
as a rosy blush
inflames cherubic cheeks

a cast-away
for she has taken your place
mastering the heavens
up in outer-space
a show and tell
along with a gathered grace
protecting you
from the perils of confusion
and undue haste

plentiful words spoken
dripping syllables
dismembered and broken
arming yourself against
what has not been said
a slight trace
of admiration and love
suddenly revoked
by the gods
who loom up above

a rambunctious hug
and a slither of a touch
smooth skin paving the way
for the chance to repay
another unforgiveable sin
always ready and waiting
for him

never giving up hope
for you have always balanced
your love life
on an uneven tightrope
groundbreaking seconds
making your stomach sink
as you breathlessly stare
at his profound and sexy wink

A BONE TO PICK

an intrusive tongue
dripping saliva
into your mouth
enough tears shed
along with an inkling
of a doubt
momentarily remembering
what he is all about
as a tastier version
of the past
repeats itself through
insurmountable words
which crumble and spill
an agonizing task
soon to be completed
as a troubling notion
forcibly opens a mouth
of foaming incoherence

GIRLS' CLUB

a perplexing brow
dripping sweat
upon her
golden crown
cheery, bright highlights
dragging her down
long braids
secured with
rainbow-colored,
elastic bands
black and white ribbons
which lend a hand
a sour, lemon drop
placed in her mouth
by her best friend
who has been
living without
trading her licorice
and gumballs
for smiling dolls
drilled together
with barb-wire
and plastic stars
a colorful,
made-up mouth
extricating awe
from a sullen frown
robust cheeks
pink and flushed
as they compliment
a manic decision
dressing up life-like,
miniature children
in short dresses
and long skirts

an exquisite vision
entailing a variety
of girls' toys
unbefitting
a little boy

A PERFECT SOMEONE

escaping all common sense
as you deal with
quivering loins
gasping for breath
and flinging
torn stockings and coins
a waxed, shiny floor
making way for bra straps
which are released
and then ignored
inhaling
his minty breath
as saliva drips down
the side of your head
stumbling backwards
on top of him
as you laugh
never interested
in what he has to say
making small talk
in order to
stop him from
walking away
a king-size bed
and scrunched-up sheets
shifting in the summer heat
sheer curtains
billowing in the breeze
as you search for your clothes
and ask him to leave

A WEIGHTY ISSUE

Santa climbing down
your chimney to stay
for a cup of hot cocoa
and a bit of cinnamon,
crumb cake
a rising force
lifting himself up
from a comfy, reclining chair
ordering you about
in your house slippers
without a doubt or a care
in the world for
your dilapidated house
and run-on bills
which always seem to get lost
in the stampede and shuffle
of heavy feet and uninviting thrills
a winter storm brewing
over your dainty, tea cup
always afraid to make
a sound or a yelp
flinging his hat
up into the air
as a frigid, freeze warning
constitutes a consuming stare
a whopping potbelly
overlapping faded overalls
as food plasters itself
onto his snowy, white shawl
a mustache filled with crumbs
from his evening rounds
slipping and falling
from the momentous force
of his raging pounds

BURSTING YOUR BUBBLE

a pin-sized needle
deflating a
robust balloon
a voluptuous,
beaming mass
exploding
inside of you
enraptured color
vibrant as
silver dollars
hanging from
an unraveling thread
as you scream
and holler

CROSSING THE LINE

about to ruin
a perfect evening
as you slowly
undress him
while staring up
at the ceiling
trying to disarm
yourself quickly
for you are helplessly
knocked out
flailing and sinking
an unfortuitous turn
of events
turning you into
a desperate wretch
a build-up
of nervous anticipation
and stomach upset
experiencing a bout
of regret
as you sidestep
illicit trouble
firmly pressing
your chin up
against his
growing stubble

IN LIMBO

smoky, black eyes
rimmed with
designer eyeliner
not once, but twice
a formidable disposition
aching for the revival
of the once smitten
remembering being held
in his arms
like a soft,
furry kitten

a desirous peace
overcoming you
as you flip through
fashion magazines
and what have you
wondering if your hair
looks okay
as a straggly piece
whips itself
in front of your face

a damaged complexion
hidden underneath makeup
which sticks
to an unhealthy obsession
massive oils which
make you look
sultry and trim
a vast array of products
meant to slow down
the aging process
peering into mirrors
reflecting a broad face
and a clever, curling iron

for you could never
get enough of him
his endearing smile
and light-filled eyes
suddenly turning dim
a sigh escaping
the closest call
as you seethe underneath
his quiet scrutiny
never one to make
small talk
out of a righteous
and cordial duty

no one else will ever do
as you hide behind
a messy up do
dark and dampened shadows
perfecting dazzling stars
which twinkle
tight-fitting clothes
still pasted on your form
minus all the wrinkles

a tidbit of
good-willed advice
making headway through
another tumultuous lie
a bitter unrest consuming you
as you wait for him
to make the next move

ONCE AS A CHILD

a pastel pink, cotton dress
floating above her
uneven, tan ankles
profound movements
of animated joy
as she wraps her arms around
her brand new toy

a disheveled appearance
rehashing a child-like innocence
long, drawn-out days
of make-believe
encompassing a full repertoire
of fun and games
jovial smiles and silly jokes
remembering when
you were small
the exhilarating time
before adult life
has taken its toll

a shriek and a cry
as she jumps up into
the vibrant, blue sky
jumping jacks and hopscotch,
candy corn,
and chocolate, pop tarts
wishing to relive days
of pure happiness
before the ill-fated discovery
of difficult and painful sustenance

GRIN AND BEAR IT

a tower of strength built
in order to sustain
a level of indifference
calculating questions
which are nagging
and persistent
a cold, sinister peace
wrapping you up within
plush blankets
which cry out
raging disbelief
a slow intoxication
of brandy
and a heartfelt concession
of grief
exaggerated words
and loud cursing
just say
what you have to say
and get on with it
for an evasive explanation
awaits
for every twinkling star
which forms
an unbiased attitude
adopted
ever since you were born

COLD FEET

discarding a puckered,
wedding dress
baby-blue garters
and strategically-placed lace
columns of long organza
trailing behind
your favorite mate
as swirls of
soft, luxurious silk
are stitched together
in due haste
crystal goblets
clinging and shattering
while numerous voices
ask you
what is the matter
sipping a divine concoction
entailing a berry and melon twist
a sparkling champagne
which tantalizes and insists
gathering up your wits
to graciously welcome
a classic and divine institution
painstakingly arranged
for those ready to witness
a concrete absolution
a numbing force
catapulting you onward
wooden pews
which are dressed up
in a bright array
of pastel hues
nervously crying out
as a lingering feeling
of doubt turns into
an overwhelming effort
sustained in order to
please a crowd

SALVATION'S STORM

slamming your car
in reverse
as you back up
and curse
weightless snow
which doodles
and then draws
fiery winds
howling and screaming
their upcoming dread
as swirls of fury
paw at you instead
a flurry or two
bombarding your
fleece-lined boots
digging your hands
into deep pockets
of your insulated,
ski suit
finally giving in
to his snide
and rude remarks
a juvenile arrogance
and conceit
demeaning her
from the very start
sunken shores
and vast,
opulent beaches
surrendering
to a higher degree
of being
for you have
hopelessly dreamed
of when and where
you might meet him

PAST YOUR PRIME

having not a care in the world
a stone-cold face and
chiseled cheekbones
a fiery light snuffed out
of a welcoming and vivid night
concrete, blank walls
unreadable and hard to ignore
as canvases of white
urge you to draw

the time for worthless conclusions
have come and gone
relying heavily upon
all that has been spun
out of crocheted sweaters
and knitted scarves
a corduroy jacket
covering tired
and muscled limbs
instigating a revival of
beaten, weather conditions

a cold and frigid morning
light and mellow
despite a heavy heart
and a raging peril
doubtful reassurances
slipping and sliding
through times of fleeting
reoccurrences
a strong endurance
catching up with a fluid
and emotionless current

deciding to push onwards
as if she never existed
thick stacks of newspapers
and tall words becoming useless
letters left unopened
as you throw away
your last chance of wanton survival
terminating a torrid relationship
which has never been required

a riveting tale of heartache
finally pushed away
as another introduction
makes vast headway
showered with exhaustion and relief
for you are soon to be set free
only to realize that
she could never be me

LEAVING HIS MARK

pungent evergreens
and maple leaves
reaching for
a turbulent
and navy sea
a harsh rumbling
of the earth
as you glance
gray, storm clouds
which churn
a wavering disbelief
for you can never
get a grip on
his dastardly deeds
unable to forgive him
his everlasting,
dirt marks
on your sleeve
a pre-shrunk variety
of cotton,
short-sleeve tees

POSTER BOY

demeaning your stature
by studying one
who is buff and natural
self-serving
is an idyllic frame
a worthless sham
incorporating a global shame
inquiring about
a broad and muscular man
plastered on poster board
high above glittering lights
and a moonlit ball
a gruff exterior
featuring a supreme,
noble cause
as he stoically stands
straight and tall
taking you by surprise
is a juicy tidbit
embarrassed and ashamed
as you watch him
flex and rip
a potent energy
waxing and waning
as stars in your eyes
sparkle and inflame
strolling through
shopping malls
a pretentious neighborhood
full of upscale stores
a larger-than-life score
inhabiting glass windows
and doors

A MALE VARIETY

blissfully unaware
of leering eyes
a pencil-thin skirt
clinging to her
shapely thighs
searching for another
with whom
to playfully covet
a feminine, thought process
possessing a woman
who will inevitably suffer
willing to make amends
for an unforgiveable mistake
tearfully begging
as he decides
to raise the stakes
doubting the validity
of her apology
for he will
always question
her attempts
to entice those
of an available,
male variety

A NIBBLE

a sweet and salty fix
pieces of granola
and walnuts
added to the mix
slowly biting into
a crunchy substitute
for melting butter
and tangy licorice

a blissful state
encountering a
heavenly relief
for you are resolved
never to cheat
endlessly hoping
to consume
a cream-filled cheesecake

wanting to kick yourself
as you crave salt and sugar
chocolate frosting and
a flame-broiled burger
tasty condiments added
despite a strong will
reaping havoc
upon the svelte appearance
of miniscule pounds
for he will inevitably succumb
to her tasty treats
when you are not around

strong, yet sad
as you mistake
anger for fear
a secret yearning
for you have waited
all year
a holiday bash
and extravaganza

luring you away
from a peace-filled day
a constricting throat
unused to having your say

a buffet table full of
appetizers and nibblers
happily munching on
mini foodstuff and cake
forcing yourself not to cave
for you have always
been jealous
of other women
who keep themselves
in shape

a dessert table
reserved just for you
as you contemplate
burying yourself
within enticing depths
of a chocolate, sundae goo
fighting the urge
to devour and splurge
as you undo buttons
of your bulging pantsuit

A SPECTATOR'S WOE

in close contact
with a glamorous girl
grabbing your attention
are silky ringlets of curls
windblown hair
swirling and twirling
around rigid shoulders
an entrancing vision
encouraging you
to get to know her
a broad back insistent
on leading the way
through long aisles
and faces
which peer attentively
at a dimly-lit stage
a drama unfolding
as the curtain rises
enthralled with flashes of color
decorating long gowns
with dignified collars
a spectator's woe
urging you to sit
in a plush seat
leaning back
with your head down
as you slip into a silent retreat
fighting to stay awake
as you silently debate
whether you are
entitled to a long,
overdue break
a boring overture
facing a clock
which ticks ever-so-slow
coming to a compromise
as you both get up to go

CHIPPER AND DAP

an acknowledgement
worthy of a thousand words
a charismatic drawl echoing
as you politely ask for more
a tempting cocktail
wrapped up
within napkins
soaked to the rim
a lingering scent
evaporating
at the sight of him

experiencing a
nervous anticipation
and a slight trepidation
as you take a chance
and slowly
dance with him
mimicking his steps
as you inhale
his fragrant scent
a celebration
to be held in his honor
as the man of the hour
exhibits a raw
and delicious power
expensive cashmere
coveting a neckline
undeserving of his
inquisitive eyes
a scintillating, self-worth
plummeting
as you fall by the wayside

a decadent dance
and a sizzling romance
lively music blaring
as you shed your disguise
along with a long, tiered dress

ruffles and intrinsic lace
tripping you
as you fall from grace
losing your footing
at the most
inopportune time
and place

a distinguished gentleman
hiding a gruff interior
for you are caught mumbling
at his chipper and dap exterior
pretending to be comfortable
with an undeserving event
for he is unworthy
of all precious time spent

READY

a prowess
attacking him
seething words
sinking in
a burning
re-entrance
into his world
confronting him
with evidence
incriminating
another girl
a pivotal awakening
making you shake
and scream
a volatile heart
ready for
almost anything

AUTHOR GARB

whistling a tune
as you hum yourself
out of bed
at half past noon
lifting your arms
up off your thighs
as you stifle
a shriek and a cry

stumbling
as you stub your toe
on the edge
of a bureau drawer
trailing behind you
is a warm coverlet
caught in-between
a cotton blanket
are dark,
paisley threads

sneaking a peek
into the living room
as you wipe
the last remnant of sleep
from your cheek
bone-chilling nightmares
waking you up
before you are
hungry enough to eat

huffing and puffing
as you toss away
scribbled sentences,
stacks of sheets,
and random thoughts
misconstrued
getting ready to
write another story
as you contemplate

becoming
focused and renewed
mismatched attire
reserved just for you
as you throw on
an old, ratty tee shirt
stained with splotches
of drool

fumbling around
for a hair tie
pulling yourself together
by securing
your stringy hair up high
smudges of mascara
creasing and caking
around the darkened
perimeters of your eyes

BECOMING ANGEL

wrestling underneath
soft, polyester sheets
a drip-dry fabric
measuring only about
waist-deep
slipping and sliding
over slim ankles
and devout wrists
a pounding ocean
raging through
your stunned lips

ice-cold and tingling
a rush of cold
and heat simmering
permitting you to persist
within his raging kiss
a slight breeze
blowing in your ears
as fluctuating waves
soar high and crash
into sinful
and tantalizing bliss

an angel walking steadily
over bricks and nails
a blurry, tunnel vision
threatening to fail
aching to see past his
muscled and corded spine
grasping at straws
and running out of time

sharp angles
and soft, swollen limbs
shaking uncontrollably
as he gives in
your true intent
swaying underneath

a cordial countenance
and a heavenly sign
contemplating the many reasons
why he shouldn't be mine

a torrid avalanche
of emotions
coming and going
as you wear your heart
on your sleeve
a bitter unrest turning into
a naked and brave reprieve
trying to enable his heart
to slow down and just be
as you flag down his ship
to overcome your mighty sea

TOOLING LEATHER

crafty and aged hands
indented wrinkles
which withstand
an enormous amount
of artistic ability
grasping a piece
of tan leather
along with all of his
tooling artillery
laying complacent in his lap
are sheets of buffalo silk
and deer mink
enough to assemble
a long, striking coat
leather bands and buttons
thoughtfully scripted
from long-ago
discovering a smooth foundation
of plentiful, velvety textures
a plausible separation
into four or more sections

a rueful grimace
appearing on
his compelling face
transforming miniature pieces
of rawhide
into what would have been
an unnecessary waste
become a transitory,
earthbound soul
whose fervor is pronounced
only when he is
courageous and bold
the gift of being
enormously clever
while sticking to his ideals
even through
the thickest of weather

pondering what it will take
to gather up all his materials
into a trusted, enormous heap
an iconic hero
with enough perseverance
to complete
a vast array of artistic endeavors
a smoldering passion required
in order to excel
at the craft
of tooling leather

DUSTING COBWEBS

a haggard face
entailing dirty,
face-framing layers
a torrid biography
hidden within her
obnoxious behavior
a needy woman
who has survived
the most vicious
of storms
tumbling into adverse,
weather conditions
as roadblocks
delay her progress
into the unknown

A NIGHT TERROR

a tap on the shoulder
and an eagle's cry
making you bolt upright
with dubious surprise
studying each ray of light
as it surpasses
a fearful midnight
the gossamer threads
of a dream
interrupted within the midst
of a slight tremor and scream
peeking over your shoulder
as a mounting intuition
and gut instinct take over
a ghastly turn of events
urging you to consider
what exists beyond
the five senses
shivering and shaking
from a deep chill
as you burrow underneath
thick, cotton sheets
unmoving and still

GO FLY A KITE

an ominous feeling
tearing up your insides
syncopated time
elapsing
after having been
thrown aside
the sound of her voice
reflecting summer-like
symptoms
of your choice
yearning for time
to come crawling back
through a past
resonating within waves
of sickening insight
disrupting an easy,
languid flow
as white, fluffy snow
covers your overalls
thick, leather boots
rushing through
as you glance
conspicuous colors
of her fleece-lined suit
experiencing a
mind-numbing hopelessness
and a freezing chill
working its way
into tender, aching joints
dismissing signs of frostbite
as you pursue a stick figure
grasping colorful balloons
while flying a kite

BREAD GONE STALE

untwisting a loaf of bread
as you hurriedly extract
two slices without regret
sweet and sour condiments
added to a soggy sandwich
stacked with pastrami,
Swiss cheese, and the
makings of a beef manwich

the tantalizing aroma of
grease and hamburger meat
making you crave a shot
of salt, sugar, and sweets
diving into a bag of potato chips
chosen to improve your mood
yet to decide if you should satisfy
your unforgiving, sweet tooth
with fattening comfort food

peanut butter and jelly
promising to add
a chunky layer of protein
to your already-bursting belly
unable to find a butter knife
to smear it all on
tight lids refusing to open
as you shake and bang
irritating, glass jars
until they are broken

unbaked batter
and gooey dough
quickly growing stale
for an expired loaf of bread
is unworthy of purchasing
even when it is on sale

BETTER THAN

undisclosed
is the worst
side of him
soon to appear
an alternate reality
relieving you
of your tears
pulling the wool over
your trusting eyes
as you admire
his dapper disguise
sneaking a
second look
after being hurt
for anything
is better than
what he is worth

AS THE PLOT THICKENS

a blank page
spitting vulgarities
as you rush to type
characters leading
to tragedy
a mediocre involvement
tempting a reaction
as you concentrate
on breathing
a subtle distraction
an explosion of thoughts
tearing you apart
raising your arms
above your brow
while allowing them
to doubt
a flailing redundancy
worthy of justifiable cause
a picturesque feeling
tumbling from words
which fall
run-on paragraphs
piling themselves into a heap
a tragic ending to what
you have foreseen
a ringing in your ears
followed by a jolt
of undisclosed feelings
rushing to escape
the antics of
imaginary beings

SINGLED OUT

studying your dainty feet
as you self-consciously tie
your string bikini
a smear of toothpaste
found on your cheek
as you decide to jog
down to the beach
a long stretch of sand
expecting you to withstand
brilliant rays illuminating
deep reds, yellows, and tans
delicate flowers
blooming intoxicating power
as a voluptuous design
of a woman
shifts into languid shapes,
angular features,
and delicate cheekbones
momentarily blinded
by the aging effect
of softening muscle
and a fragile ego
as you watch dusk and dawn
come together to form
an excuse for a summer storm
a volatile goddess
rising up to meet you
as you stop to breathe in
salty mildew
slowly emerging
is a ripening sunset
constituting inflamed,
yellow hair,
jolly, apple cheeks,
and an interrogating stare

SOURPUSS

the mere mention of you
will make his lush lips drool
an attempt to camouflage
his growing jubilation,
cherry cheeks,
and a slow elation

tender compliments received
as you reach for his hand
a moment of silence
as you try to comprehend
heartfelt emotion
taking precedence over
a fiery and explosive revulsion

a brilliant light
shining in his eyes
unshed tears
and a silent compromise
provoking a sullen episode
for he will try and pinpoint
what is wrong
your deep
and penetrating stare
sizing him up
for way too long

hoping for the best
as his eyes wander
from your feet
up to your breasts
a fair complexion
and a doll-like innocence
waiting for you
to drop the bomb
at this very minute

an eerie stillness
betraying his heart
with an emotionless current
a sense of hesitation
picked up by an inborn radar
and second sight
a feeling deep down
which he can never fight

unable to meet his gaze
as your mind fidgets
and then sways
turning away
from his sweet smile
suddenly turning south
a sourpuss inhabiting
a morose and
unsuspecting mouth

ON SABBATICAL

beach occupants
jumping and splashing
within deep, dark water
cavorting and laughing
a cold, harsh truth
diving into waves
which push you
into a deep reverie
brandishing
your swimsuit
on a thoughtless day
coming clean
as a swift wind
begs you to stay
bright lights
and inner-city demons
intercepting a
timeless beauty
you have vehemently
been seeking

UPSETTING THE APPLECART

reverberating,
chiming bells
resonating
all that you
have withheld
a poignant time
remembered
as he casts his spell
a sad disappointment
for he is the one
anointed
the king of your sun
a decision warranting
what should be,
said, and done
as you continuously
allow him
to put you down
unable to proceed
as usual
for he has been
upsetting the applecart
by being ruthless
and cruel
a toppling array
of bundles and sheets
thrown away
as you retreat
a displaced anger
and an emotional tyranny
hidden within
every cause
and probability
abruptly taken away
is your last chance
to reconcile

for a discouraging love
can be won back
with a fake hug
and a toothy smile

SYNCOPATION

an apocalyptic pressure
inhabiting your aching joints
a burning sensation
igniting your loins
a pompous attitude
begging to be released
as you hold
your thoughts together
with a syncopated beat

A HEAVENLY DIVERSION

swept clean
are her river-green eyes
sweltering in the summertime
along with tall glasses
of lemonade
a tangy, stinging sign
served with
sickening-sweet sugar
too hyper to stand still
leaning back as she spills
onto slick, green grass
a nerve-racking defeat
which has superimposed
her feet
onto thick, plush carpet
always spotless and clean
tidying up is wifey
in all her absolute notoriety
glasses of champagne fizzing
alongside a five-course meal
sizzling
over the noisy racket
of loud, obnoxious children
wishing to go back
to a time of peace and quiet
a heavenly diversion
minus all the hype

VACUOUS HEART

a resourceful logic
succumbing to
fiery emotions
planetary waves
striped green
and blue paisley
a gulp and a swallow
able to be borrowed
as you coast through
long, overwrought miles
a raging temptation
turning into a great,
abhorrent deviation
a vacuous heart
aching for a second chance
as you fight blissful memories
precluding
a slight, casual circumstance
the rush of crimson blood
pounding through
meandering veins
unsuccessfully crawling
towards your ultimate aim

DEPLETED

a slight wind blowing
in your ears
a poignant song captured
through a sneeze and a drone
a whimsical parody
releasing you for
the time being
a fragrant essence
taking you gently away
upon wings which spread
to invite you in
a sordid disillusion
always and forever
relating to him

practice what you preach
and try to grasp
what has always been
out of reach
power lines grounded
due to an eerie,
high-pitched squeak
a caving-in of principles
held near and dear
to your heart
forgetting that
you were here
from the very start

a weakening lethargy
holding on until
you were depleted
of life's energy
a bundle of self-worth
wasted on a man
who will never become
all that you have hoped

HOPSCOTCH

a brush of defeat
yet
always landing on your feet
a conglomeration
of thoughts and feelings
urging you to scream
your significant other
mistakenly thinking that
he will own you forever
a fading inkling of desire
disappearing without
a glimmer of hope
or rejuvenating fervor
an unsalvageable relationship
poignant in all its complexity
instigating a forceful drop
of sweltering temperature
a distant rumbling
of ferocious weather
lightning bolts acting
as an electrical conduit
an accelerating force
pulling you away
from arms
which pretend to behave
a suffocating embrace
never enough
to keep you in your place

BELL OF THE BALL

bold and courageous
a preening bell
at a lascivious gathering
glittering lights
and a disco ball
rainbow colors
and a spotlight
aiming at her
as you listen to her
quaint and southern drawl
a smooth disposition
yanking free of any opposition
for she has expended great pains
to reel him in
with a tentative gasp
she undeniably proclaims
that she will be the one
who will pull in the reins
the queen of all
scandalous, wanton games

BURNING BRIDGES

crying out
to be recognized
a sneaky peak
and a sideways glance
brown eyes wanting
to be idolized
wishing for his dreams
to come true
despite a never-ending web
of scotch tape and super glue
crinkled-up, paper balls,
scribbled notes,
and a scam of a chance
an egocentric man
able to climb through
the toughest quicksand

living in a fantasy world
is enough to make him
self-assured
a confident smile
and amazing, good looks
allowing unfortuitous days
to follow
a smorgasbord of enemies
already made
on the brink of self-discovery

DRIP-DRY

polished, black hair
threading its way
squiggly lines
linear and micro-fine
an inconsistent, baffling beauty
a makeshift, body wave protruding
an accident
waiting to happen
dubious mistakes made
while comforting him
like a brother
watching him flirt and mingle
amongst a flock
of territorial seagulls
a brooding wind calling
embarking upon a trip
on an imaginary broom
noticing the way
he looks at her
a slight fidget
and an eye-opening study
of thunderous rain
and constant gloom
incoherent thoughts racing
a mile a minute
so caught up in
an obsessed-filled heart
frantically trying to keep
drip-drying days
from tearing
cumulus clouds apart

AN IMMINENT REGRESSION

pretend you
never laid eyes on him
bright smiles
full of poking, laughing fun
looking at you
as if you were about to
keel over and spill
from the detrimental effect
of a few, miniscule pills
bitter complaints
starting to simmer
along with a hard,
penetrating glare
the demise of
blushing, pink lips
now colorless and bare

pounding on doors
of brittle, aging wood
memorizing the sight of him
as best you could
seeking refuge from
his smooth skin
a divine mixture
of sweat and sin
a slight prickle
of bereavement felt
as your body temperature rises
along with the searing heat
from hell

an illuminating effect
as you gaze at portraits
comprising stoic, winter scenes
the daring caricature
of ice-filled lakes and streams
a vibrant urgency of color
running asunder
as you frantically
pave the way
for the sultry image
of summer

A CLOSE CALL

asking for a small token
of your esteem
a flyaway high
as I reach out to grab
your silken thigh
soft murmurs passing through
our dedicated union
still trying to analyze
the potent mystery of you
a nightshift ending
as I lock heads with you
a brutal thrust
and a poignant fragrance
keeping me from
almost misbehaving
soft lips which whisper
utter decadence
while you hold me tight
wishing for one more star
to align with us tonight
an affirmation
which I could have foreseen
if you had taken the time out
to look at me
straining sideways
and behind me
as I swoop down
to retrieve the last shred
of hapless dignity
making a fool out of myself
as I replenish and rehydrate
after such a close call

THE GRAND SCHEME OF THINGS

patience wearing thin
as you procrastinate
to fit it all in
a mediocre presumption
of cheap dates and thrills
a hopeless analysis of all
that has been torn down
and rebuilt
a bitter rage
and imploding fireworks
wearing you down
unable to cry out
to all that you have succumbed
an incessant journey
of unfavorable setbacks
urging you to run
through memories
which mean nothing
to no one

RED GLOBE

a sweet, summer sizzler
making your loins quiver
a gasping strength
and over-strained limbs
a slight trace
of deodorant's stains
on tank tops
colored blue, pink, and rose
a blushing equivalent
to an angelic incident
pulling you up from
another precedence
basking in the limelight
of a hot, red globe
a boiling sun
marking its entrance
with a world-wide
glimmer of hope

a wise earth
waiting for the ones
who will succumb
to messing with it
run-down and burning lawns,
makeshift, garden sprinklers,
and the abyss
of nature's unknown
sustenance winding down
after making ill-use
of earth's resources
silently crying out in pain
are those who can hear
the clock ticking down
into an abhorrent
and senseless shame

green leaves
and a wide denial
absently reminding you
of numerous,
empty tomorrows
mouth-watering fruits
and vegetables
succumbing to a bright array
of greens, yellows, and oranges

oceans galore
and salty perfume
resonating from the
earth's floor
unable to ignore
the slow destruction
of our world
a revolting damage
unable to be fixed as before

LIGHTNING AND THUNDER

unable to break through
agonizing cries
screaming wanton lies
a round-about way
of determining a cordial sigh
a gruff exterior
encompassing little
to nothing inferior
a tolerable amusement
wondering what
he will say or do
wanting to kiss him
inviting, full lips
and a whisper of breath
in your ears
a pounding tide
and an unstoppable wave
of tears
riding high
amongst a devastating surf
forcibly pulling you under
while you take the time out
to admire an explosion
of lightning and thunder

HANGING BY A THREAD

a deep rumbling
felt within the pit
of your stomach
a quick intake of breath
as you stumble
upon a surprise
which has never
been expected
a howl and a scream
a tiny prayer entailing all
that will inevitably be
hanging by a thread
while you beg
for the courage to see

the distinct unraveling
of things
and denial floating
upon your distant moon
upmost priorities
existing at the forefront
as you patiently wait
for the striking hour of noon

a conquest
which should have been over
a long time ago
a brazen walk taken
on a thinning tightrope
a balancing act
shaking you to the core
as you repeat
the same mistakes
as before

NAIVETY

a soft chuckle
and a murmur of delight
warm, comfortable hands
slipping out of your sight
a full, pouty mouth
rolling syllables
underneath and around
a quirky sense of humor
and the fervent need
to be alone with him
a master in disguise
wrapping you around
his belittling fingers
a show and tell
for the unworldly
and the unwise
a growing spurt of naivety
disappearing
into an o-shaped mouth
a mind-boggling enigma
finally figured out

NIGHT TRAVELER

a perilous, windswept breath
breeding smoke circles
forming a halo around
a magnificent, light source
a distant evening
of twinkling lights galore
shining over your favorite city

a sugar-coated, coffee cup
grasped within gloved hands
another mistake to be had
as you fall onto
undisturbed, smooth sand
a miraculous moment experienced
for you have longed to renew
your aching sense of spirit

profoundly happy to be here
in your hometown
bursting forth
is a high and mighty energy
a long course of frenzied activity
experienced within the midst
of a magical holiday

trees covered
with a brilliant moonlight
a roaring of seas
and turbulent waves
unseasonably coming to be
an overshadowed moon
and glittering, twinkling stars
endlessly captivating you

a portrait materializing
from nights which fly by
at the speed of light
a slowing down
of movement and sound
as you unwillingly plant
your feet onto the ground

SELLING YOURSELF SHORT

a deer
caught in
headlights
embarking upon
another
disastrous plight
a stoplight
urging you
to slow down
as you helplessly
become
another object
recovered
in the lost
and found
a valued ethic
and moral code
to live by
never knowing
the reasons why
the last shred
of common sense
shed
as you reluctantly
agree
to what has just
been said

PITY PARTY

recalling days
which were fluent
and evolving
second chances
and an all-inclusive,
pity party
colorful ribbons
tied into long tresses
disheveled braids
put through
the ultimate test
a gathering of wits
and a fervent episode
of hard-earned bliss
a pivotal resurrection
and the untimely absolution
of a kiss
a nonchalant meaning
read within
non-descript words
careening
minute syllables
which fall from
a downturned mouth
invoking dreary, gray skies
which turn
the heavens south

LIFELINE

a dreaded introduction
heading towards
the ultimate destruction
meaningless words
uttered
in order to curb
distraught feelings
and hurt
a rendezvous
taking you
to times past
as poignant memories
deter
what will inevitably
happen next

WITH ALL YOUR MIGHT

parentheses surrounding
exclamatory words
paving the way
for a larger-than-life
world
stringing along
non-conforming habits
along with past loves
ruined and tragic
a torrid avalanche
and a passing whim
of seclusion
wishing for a natural habitat
to reside in
a slight breeze
pronouncing his roving eye
an absolute shame
despite a number
of inconclusive lies
putting one foot
in front of the other
as you try
with all your might
to acknowledge
all of his wrongdoings
despite being right

CHALK IT UP

a tremendous drop
in barometric pressure
dripping seconds
turning into
sullen and rainy weather
delicate sounds
and ghostly echoes
renewing a sense of shame
as you try to turn your back on
a mediocre and presumptuous game

for it is too late
reeling you in
with his smooth gait
open pores perusing
blood-thickening veins
as he claws his way
onto your delicate frame
fevered, high-pitched sounds
and an aggravating rush
chalked up to a steamy interlude
with nothing to gain
and no one to trust

an out-of-control, love affair
pulling you under
dispelling all hard-earned facts
as lightning runs asunder
an inconceivable dalliance
suspended within throes
of fevered excitement
as you rid yourself
of the unnecessary need
to keep silent

ROTTEN

rarely in for a treat
as he bombards you
with a heart
that barely beats
lackluster stars in his eyes
promises which will
never materialize
for the going will get rough
despite being made of
unyielding, unbreakable stuff

an indelible package
of skin, meat, and bones
massaging and rubbing
your itty, bitty toes
scratching nails
against torrid skin
as you experience
a wanton release with him

a discouraging circumstance
for you should have known
where he has been
a scavenger on the hunt
ready to pounce
on another scantily-clad body
basking in the sun

sizing up whatever
you thought he was
falling to pieces
and finally giving up
joyfully succeeding
in becoming the perfect fling
only to be paid back
by a rotten, human being

OUT OF YOUR NICHE

a primal instinct
holding her down
until she sinks
a wise and uninhibited woman
whose mind is as quick
as any man's
on the brink
of numerous discoveries
more than worthy
of a noble cause
a superior demeanor
waiting for her
to take the fall
an atrocious amount
of detestable feeling
merging with a
high and mighty dealing
as she suffocates
with the need to be
as important as the one
known as he
a futile glance
and the telltale signs
of a queen
outright irreverence
urging her to scream
miniature heels
clicking on glass floors
along with black-tasseled,
loafer prints
plastered on cement walls

UNMASK

a troublesome degree
of knickknacks
crumbling within your grasp
a wild notion of what will
inevitably happen next
a turnaround of thoughts
which will soon succumb
to the ultimate degree of finesse
transforming into Hercules
and conjuring up
super-human strength
in order to pass this test

a worthwhile cause
and the habitual sun
surpassing no one
gleaming rays
of a rainbow variety
urging you to believe
in a miracle yet to come
absolute notoriety
and a neutral frame of mind
a give and take cherished
with those not of your kind

a pause and a reverberation
of clicking glasses
a noisy celebration
introducing you
as a winner at last
streaming balloons
and a tasteful array
of ice cream cake
colorful tassels
hiding all your stupid mistakes

trying to misdirect
all unfavorable gloom
as you hurriedly escape
into a deserted room
more than ready to take part in
another unscrupulous game
as you try to live up to
your false, ungenuine name

RISE AND SHINE

hovering above your bed
are swirling clouds
of vanilla incense
captivating you with a strong,
intimate fragrance
preparing to fall
onto the hard-wood floor
as your cat awakens you
with his low meow
and deep moan

huddled underneath
a soft, plush comforter
hidden delicately away
from the pain and strain
of a "move faster than
you did yesterday" brain
dizzying thoughts
which can never be bought
by his solemn, timid words
bright with an age-old wisdom
until you cough

reaching for tissues
and soft, fragrant lotion
blowing your nose
to rid yourself
of his cosmic pollution
a strain of the common cold
encompassing all the nights
it took to recall
a star-crossed lover
you had inadvertently
fallen for

a rise and shine
on a clear, fall day
giving rise to
an unobstructed view
of colorful leaves and trees
casting its magical spell upon you
as you heed the morning's
polite request
to remain free of any activity
having to do with uninvited guests

the same, old tune
drifting through hi-fi speakers
as you duck for cover
your loving cat
burrowing his head deep
into your lap
soft whiskers tickling your cheek
as you rush to rise
for an early-morning,
breakfast treat

BLAMELESS

a single prayer
spoken quietly
underneath it all
exhaling loudly
a nonplussed episode
and a winding road
leading the way through
mud-thickening snow
dreary, gray footprints
stomping through
thigh-high snowdrifts
making headway
since you became
unafraid
to mince words
a grave heart
accelerating at
a furious speed
blinded by
incessant rage
and explosive fury

CLOSET MANIAC

a proven incident
worthy of a thousand overtures
beaming accolades
and long hair to uncurl
an offer of assistance
and obliging words
echoing through
two, different worlds
a perfunctory win
as you place his hands
where you can see them
a crumbling defeat
for you have always
believed him
dirty whispers
echoing in an alleyway
marked by rotting splinters,
gray cement,
and belligerent rain
paying the price
for thinking he is
an honest man
measuring up to the top
of a measly, coke can
aiming higher than
what he wants you to be
a closet maniac
worthy of being anything other
than what you speak

FANNING FLAMES

gaping wounds,
bleeding guts,
and someone new
a heart
disgruntled
and raw
still fanning
flames
of long ago

A HEAD START

barely escaping
the shadowy edges
of noon
a tempting proposal
resurfacing
after leaving so soon
a head start
embarked upon
as you wave goodbye
to the sight
of no one
partaking in
a favorable form
of communication
as desolate arms
embrace a
welcoming,
morning sun

LONE WOLF

jumbled, mixed messages
and a hair's breath
of disruptive influences
constantly urging you
to throw in the towel
forfeiting lively illusion
paving the way
for illuminating midnight
shining its rays
into clouded eyes
a constant upheaval
minus the questions why
a bold and courageous feat
called for
as you gather your wits
and call the shots
standing your ground
while curiously watching
everyone else
sink and then drown
a strung-out crowd
urging you
to remain calm
discouraging you
from making
a peep or a sound

GIVE IT A REST

inhaling the scent
of honeybee tea
as dripping teabags
introduce a
new possibility
cumulus clouds
hovering over
your backyard swing
as ramshackle sheds
ache to be cleaned
a glorious day
stumbled upon
as you
let your hair down
reminiscing within
a soothing breeze while
ferociously devouring
scorching degrees of heat
crystal, blue water
and relaxing waves
beach towels
and a soggy mess
to save
rivers sabotaging
reality's quest
for you only
have a minute
to sit down and rest

HIGHEST HONOR

an indomitable spirit
confused by utter incoherence
trailing behind is
a make-believe mind
wishing to beseech
more of his kind
engrossed within
predetermined times
and the bold introduction
of a magical,
exquisite visit
tolerating it all
for only about
an hour and a minute
the mere mention
of gullible words
and his signature phrases
you have studiously learned
recognizing and ignoring
the decadent thrill
of the unseen world
a roller-coaster ride
of twists, turns, and spills
acknowledging what
has been said
as he tries to lure you
back into bed
nightlights twinkling
throughout a midnight,
summer fling
rewarded
the most highest of honors
without doing a thing

A PUSH AND A SHOVE

a sufficient amount
of evidence needed
in order for you
to bow down
and retrieve it
frivolous documentation
and the chance
to believe him
another pitiful
acknowledgement
seething
after his intentional slight
devastated and hurting
after a magical
and dream-filled night

staring at
a skim, frothy cappuccino
subtly placed in front of you
as you dictate your thoughts
onto paper and chew
the end of your pen
which is brand new
flimsy excuses
entailing all which
has to be done
to end your excursion
circling around a deceptive
and simmering sun

brown eyes
leaking crystal tears
as gray circles
drip the darkest of fears
pushing and shoving
your way out from underneath
his stoic form
fervently proclaiming
that he loves only her
now and forever more

INTERCOASTAL

quaint, small-town shops
and an eastern seaboard
of vacant beaches
and docks
nostalgic ingredients
never missing
their magic touch
a salty fragrance
reminding you
of where you have been
windblown hair
and a seaside retreat
a rising, summer day
full of spicy
and succulent treats
tantalizing aromas
wafting through
cozy restaurants
and bars
a delightful distraction
as you grasp
your knife and carve
fillets of fish
and enormous shrimp
always having
enough room for
a cordial,
after-dinner mint

KLUTZ

foreign and ancient
salt and pepper shakers
adding a splash of color
to your kitchen placement
delicate, china plates
and denim-blue patterns
complimenting
expensive silverware
crocheted tablecloths
withstanding wear and tear
as you grope the banister
on your way down
the stairs
a late-dinner call
beckoning ringing bells
jingling as you fall
crystal goblets shattering
onto a shiny, wood floor

HIS FOLLY

going against a grain
of common sense
as you wag your finger
in opposition to her
once-in-a-lifetime
chance
holding her back
will never do you
any good
for you are already
lost at sea
always and forever
misunderstood
your resisting body
tingling while you
kiss her
blossoming cheeks
ripe as cherries
and angular features
sharp and full of life
indiscreetly becoming
her darling
without an argument
or a fight
mistaken as one
who never gave a damn
sabotaged by her ability
to take a leap
and a stand
forceful illusions
embedded within
a lucid landscape
of floating conclusions
suddenly taking
a turn for the worse
as you sleep with her

ignoring the concept
of right and wrong
as delicate droplets of rain
brave a new storm

A WORD FROM THE WISE

foaming at the mouth
as she drips drool
down a pathway
heading south
raging fireworks
which rip, roar, and hurl
a brutal succession of words
vacating the heart
of a troubled girl

wishing to give her
helpful advise
for she never looked at
another man twice
caving in to him
more than once
as he forces his way
into her heart
a colorful arrangement
of flowers
and a midnight collection
of stars

wasting time as you try
to talk sense into her
your friend
who never wasted
words on you
desperately speaking
your mind
for she would have done
the same in kind
making you out
to be the one
who is a worthless piece
of slime

never knowing
when to give up
for you should have
remained uninvolved
from the very start
always sticking your nose
into her business
forcing you to glow
with a cosmic and
volatile indifference

pointing out
the negative attributes
of her man
numerous phrases
and words
thrown back at you
by way of a systematic
and vengeful plan
crawling back to him
no matter what
you say or do
a bitter irony
as you remember
all that you
have been through

MESSING WITH PERFECTION

a soft and curvy form
lying in bed
with both feet up
off the floor
shaking your head
as you allow
blonde, wispy layers
to lead you
up and at 'em
instead

a long, tiresome day
entailing dreary work
and gifted,
mathematical skills
computing left to right
as command prompts
and enter keys
continuously give
you a fright

waiting for the day
to start
so you can be seen
as witty and smart
crisp, white shirts
and harsh creases
ironed out
only when they needed it

a designer suit
imitating a sharp,
military style
as rows of buttons
make it difficult to zip
up and down
fully alert
and smiling
only when the boss
is around

an educated woman
doing all that she can
while making herself
into the image
of a self-absorbed,
egotistical man

UNSCRUPULOUS

setting a good example
was never your forte
a disastrous result
forcing you
to run and then pray
a miniature flashlight
casting shadows
along deserted highways
fluorescent snow
filling up boot prints
forming uneven, gaping holes

a road map
detailing intelligible lines,
scratch paper, and receipts
crinkled due to
unscrupulous secrets
unopened, love letters
waiting for you to
grab a fortuitous situation
by the collar
dressed-up jeans
and tailored shirts
which cost hundreds of dollars

trying to trick her
into believing
that your intentions are
honorable and decent
a tangled, spider web
entailing spools
of intricate lace and thread
daring her to say anything else
than what has already
been said
her gentle letdown
persuading you to quit
while you are still ahead

TRIPLE SCOOP

a gooey, triple scoop
vanilla and fudge
dripping onto your fingertips
wanting to wipe it off
without having to lick it
a plastic spoon
waiting to be dipped
into a soft-serve cone
toppings which should
never be consumed
all alone

a mind-numbing, chocolate race
inhabiting a smooth, winter's plate
rainbow sprinkles spilling
along with coconut chips
and a fudge filling
cookie dough and rampant flavors
fooling you into believing that
everything will remain the same
as you embark upon
another sweet
and sugary plain

YOUNG CHAMP

lifting the spirits
of a young man
a childhood full
of counterfeit money
and short memorandums
a quick note and
scribbled, pen marks
doodling as he shows you
how the world works
taught to ignore
benign hurt and oozing sores
a boisterous crowd and
baseball bats reserved
for one and all
for there was
nobody around
to congratulate him
when he scored

a coincidence
or so it seemed
remembering miniature,
balled-up fists
which fought and careened
dimpled cheeks
and a softly-curved mouth
giving way to
brash wailing and screaming
sucking his thumb and pouting
is an adorable child
worth every effort
so he can be

all that he wanted to dream
in a world where
he had a chance to
become or do as he has seen
never throwing a tantrum
so he can hide
behind a pungent
bottle of wine

shortened breaths and gasps
coming in short bursts
as he sags
ignoring all the warning signs
as he whispers
a silent, thank you
to his dad

mimicking his father
as he rises
amongst the most
influential man of his day
a thin fabric caught in-between
a chance to submit
or to be treated as prey
his flag will fly no matter
how many times
he is denied
a treacherous way of life
permanently scarring him
not once, but twice

BUBBLY

a vote of confidence
is all it took
to recognize
her trembling limbs
as she shook
with unrequited lust
temptation
which has been thrust
before her eyes
a calming effect
stretching far and wide
the breadth
of his shoulder blades
and the wide expanse
of his back
denying times
of the most, profound importance
dipping and spinning
her around
upon heavenly shores
and glittering, dance floors
disco balls which reflect
rainbow lights and lost souls
a thumping, bass beat
making her heart pound
with reverberations,
eye-candy, and tasty treats
another round
of chiming glasses
clicking and crying
a sparkling bottle of bubbly
casting a spell
without even trying

HOLDING HIS OWN

crashing
upon your shore
are broken,
shattered seashells
digging into
swollen feet
as you
encourage him
to speak
a mouth
full of
sea-salt
and dangling limbs
which flail
when caught
a sea urchin
frantically trying
to breathe
held captive by
tattered,
fishing nets
and tangled
seaweed

APPEARING AS IF

appearing as if
you are too good
for this
a comical act
as you clench your fists
throwing a tantrum
knowing that
she will inevitably resist
your advances
a show and tell
reserved for those
receiving a bold kiss
the night which
has just begun
swirling music
and a disco sun
a poignant rendition
of your favorite song
casting out
lascivious evils
of her treacherous gown
a bold step taken
as she sways
in your arms
a knock-out
only when you chose
to come around
temptations fraught
with an undeniable urge
to retreat
and then withdraw
a lonely countenance
tangled up in sheets
bare and solo
appearing as if
you yearn to become
a part of a handsome
and envied duo

FOR WHAT IT WAS WORTH

revamping your image
to one which is
sullen and vintage
crocheted, hand-knit sweaters
unraveling threads
and an ongoing lineage
discarding flashy
and inappropriate clothing
never to be worn again
always wondering
what has become of him
a self-confidence
which has come and gone
tricked into believing
that you were
the only one
his deceitful intentions
for blasted, good fun
coercing you
to place yourself
on the same page
as his new girlfriend
barely escaping
with yourself intact
for he tried so hard
to manipulate you
into giving him more
than what you had

UNHAPPILY EVER-AFTER

black and blue bruises
turning into shades
of vivid pinks and blues
a screech and a cry
as a substantial bit
of evidence
works its way
down her spine
caking around
the edges
of half-closed lids
is a smoky remnant
of black liquid
blood-red eyes
and a crushing defeat
forming a puddle of spit

a begrudging crankiness
and an outpouring
of grief
grabbing soft tissue
so she can blot
her cheeks
rose-colored blush
forming harsh creases
frowning after
another one
of his long,
disconcerting speeches

a time-out
from a glaring night
makeup mirrors
reflecting an interminable
and stinging sight
a large fist and an
immediate response
to cringe
as she tries to protect her
leathery and tawdry skin

AN UNINVITED GUEST

an ominous tingling
creeping up your spine
an abrupt halt
of humming and hissing
the spit and crackle
of pounding rain
encouraging your feet
to trespass
upon someone else's domain
a sinister house spiraling
smoke and steam
a harsh temperature drop
as water trickles
down the drain
a breakout of goose bumps
and a howling, doorbell ring
forcing you to acknowledge
what you have seen
agonizingly waiting
to be pushed up
against the wall
an exasperated sigh
making you feel
vulnerable and small
a terror-stricken place
which will never
leave a trace
imaginary claws
digging themselves
into a pale
and frightened face

STICK FIGURES

a quick slash
of your pen
a stigmata
which stains
inkless men
magic markers,
crayola crayons,
and colored,
construction paper
torn and ripped
to shreds
as lonely, stick figures
occupy your bed
a duplicate man
concocted from
essential herbs,
fragrant oils,
and glycerin soap
popsicle sticks
and crazy glue
used to erect
miniature homes

HIGH INTENSITY

rising above the call of duty
as you sift and stir
a concoction blended
by yours truly
a flavorful mess
rehydrating your limbs
after a long
and disconcerting test
a justifiable movement
of arms and limbs
dedicating yourself
to a regimen of exercise
and stylish decorum

essential nutrients digested
as you swallow an enriched,
vitamin drink
a taste of honey and lemon
adding a burst of energy
to sweetened, herbal tea
sweeping your emotions
up your sleeve
as an ideal substitution
is administered
to try and help you sleep

a chance to burn
an exorbitant amount
of calories
crossing the finish line
while welcoming
the upcoming holiday
sweat and tears shed
as you work diligently
to fit into smaller clothing
a leaner physique
finally granted
due to all your
boisterous moaning

fruitfully benefitting from
a high-intensity dream
for you wish to become
part of an
award-winning team
taking a minute
to gather your wits
as you surrender
to an inhuman strength
and gift
feeling slightly bereft
after experiencing
an outpouring of
smoldering humidity
and dripping sweat

SINKING SHIP

reaching for
his frigid hand
never worthy
of being your man
a trip through time
remembering what
it felt like
to be momentarily blind
his cheap talk and lies
garrulous complaints
and empty, blank eyes
picking up the pieces
after he has made you
feel indecent
blinded by his tall,
statuesque frame
luscious lips
conversing with the gods
while addressing them
by name
an obstruction
blocking illogical thinking
from a fortunate drowning
and sinking
a desperate plea
escaping from a mouth
which can't stop screaming

PREVIOUSLY UNRELEASED

deemed necessary
is a change of heart
a sparkling accessory
glamorizing all
which has fallen apart
china-pattern dishes
engraved with a
gold, filigree design
toppling over
and exploding
into distinct pieces
of his kind
grasping his wrist
as you stop and stall
waiting for the right time
to grab onto him and claw
your way out of
a self-absorbed existence
planning to accept
his smoldering kiss
as you stumble upon
an earth-shattering bliss
never as sure as you are now
to want to get involved
a situation which will
inevitably turn sour
after being
momentarily absolved
a subtle insinuation
and a moment
to pause and reflect
deep, dark secrets
purposefully unrevealed
as of yet

DINING ALFRESCO

bailing you out
of a winter storm
with a soft caress
and an indulgent moan
a feather-light snowflake
trickling down
as a consuming restlessness
abounds
deciphering his sweet talk
as verbal clues
floating aimlessly
as you snooze
a trick of the light
illuminating shadows
of an unforgiving night
toasting marshmallows
over red, hot flame
embarrassed and ashamed
as you call out his name
the acrid scent
of burning timbers
surrounding a haven
meant to be all-inclusive
plastic forks and spoons
dipped into a savory meal
tempting you
to salivate and swoon
over meat and potatoes

GIFT OF GAB

foaming at the mouth
as your counterpart
gurgles and spews
a backlashing of words
voraciously studied
and perused
a ceaseless center
and an undermining doubt
as the minute hand
on your wristwatch
slowly heads south

a roll of your eyes
and an exasperated,
impatient sigh
mindlessly adrift
as you silently cry
watching her lips twitch
as she persists
with a whining voice
never insisting
on hearing her choice

difficult woes
and a begotten push
fighting to stay awake
for you really didn't want
to hear an obsessive dialogue
consisting of mundane waste

taking a minute to
gather your thoughts
so you can advise her
without making her sore
cultivating a meaningful way
to hide your unrest
as you try to escape her
angry protest

a loud ringing
of your cell phone
interrupting a sordid,
wasteful drone
a rambling complaint
and moan
coming from a bitter woman
who just can't leave it alone

BORN AND BRED

born to request
a thick loaf
of Italian bread
a garlic vinaigrette
adding a zing
to an already-tasty
spread

hot butter dripping
onto lace tablecloths
as linen napkins
wipe splotches of food
from the fancy dress
you bought

the complexity
of a five-course meal
reserved for
an outstanding
and uppity clientele
whose gaping mouths
deliver a big spiel

wineglasses brimming
with an old-world persuasion
as mouth-watering aromas
permeate a dining hall
full to capacity
with all your relations

TO DO OR NOT TO DO

appreciative of all
direct insinuations
a flattery
which has adorned you
with a headache
and a lack
of substantial meaning
overthrowing all
you have believed in
as you rip apart
an already torn
and broken heart
restlessly waiting
for an obsessive affair
to start
as a blinding spark
and the inability to see
dictates what will
inevitably be
a deception
overcoming
a lack of futility
while feigning
oblivion's sleep
shining upon
a twinkling star
are misgivings
floating high
while studied
from afar

NOOK AND CRANNY

creaking boards,
splitting gaps,
and gaping holes
nooks and crannies
encompassing her
dresser drawer
dividers and fillers
halting your progress
as you tuck and fold
a raglan sweater
crisscrossing beams
and a high, cathedral ceiling
disrupting an altered
state of being
an illuminating nightlight
turning a sunny day
into a star-lit night
as colorful caricatures
of giraffes and elephants
pave the way
for a soon-to-be inhabitant
a cherubic baby
shifting on your knee
as you hum her a lullaby
and watch her sleep

PINPRICK

instinctively knowing
that you are better off
without him
a devastating force
reliving all that
has been lost
a silent battle
of wills
and a face
remaining impassive,
silent, and still
deciding to ignore
open arms
as a venomous
retaliation forms

a resolute stance
and a hardened heart
reliving sordid
circumstance
a steel backbone
entailing a love life
which has
fallen short
hating him
for he is to blame
starting over again
just to be engulfed
by beseeching flame

NARCISSISTIC BLEND

a narcissistic blend
of an uptight,
conservative man
the reigning in
of sarcastic reply
and an angry
condemnation
reserved for
all those who apply
forecasting false sentiment
as you slowly
become unglued
another demeaning
remark
cultivating itself
inside of you

a chiseled, bitter
countenance
derived from aged,
putrid stone
an idyllic portrait
defining classic features
and a robust nose
ironed-out creases
and designer shirts
decorated with
tiny creatures
loose buttons
and silk thread
added on as
special features

the abhorrent way
he has treated you
his stylish haircut
and designer shoes
picking up after him
after you have been
faithful and true
destroying a
strong-willed persona
while erasing
all original thought
succumbing to
disenchantment
as you inevitably
grow soft

IMPENDING MAELSTROM

slamming your brakes
as you careen towards
an abrupt halt
a destructive, driving force
unloading frazzled thoughts
reaching for an aspirin
to help alleviate
minor pain
slowly accumulating
the strength needed
to remedy a scattered
and confused brain
fumbling for your seatbelt
while cursing your opponent
swerving out of the way
as you preach to blame
a sickening thud resonating
as you tightly grasp
a steering wheel
shocks and cylinders
shaking from your
high-pitched squeal
locked doors
urging you to open up
and get out on all fours
silently pleading for help
as oozing blood pours
from chafed and sprained elbows

MIXED MEDIA

signing your name
a scrawling signature
doodles and circles
accentuating
miniscule syllables
hands which slip
from black-ink pens
flippantly ignoring
the advances
of other men
a territory
unbeknownst to you
twisting the cap
off a tube of crazy glue
pasting pictures of him
in a scrapbook
available to eyes
which seek the truth
a creased, uneven texture
leaving their mark
upon blank canvas
a reluctant image emerging
while capturing the essence
of his undoing
acrylic paints
and a variety
of art forms
needed to portray
the exquisite vision
of his porcelain face

BUILDING BLOCKS

hunched over while
intently studying
a soon-to-be,
picture form
angular shapes
absorbing your
concentration
as you fumble
with pieces
lost without a home
a subtle intuition
guiding you
as you section off
varying sizes
of cardboard
indeterminate themes
and borders
persuading you
to meander away
from self-imposed boredom
along for the ride
is a fierce determination
building blocks used
to a solve a
mind-boggling equation
letters and numbers
strewn across your
living room floor
counting to ten
while crawling away
from all the pieces
you have thrown

HOOKED

a torrential downpour
and hurricane winds
which blow
causing you
to drown
within his undertow
time which ticks
slowly on by
with a slight tremble
and reminiscent sigh
packing your bags
filled with
lingering memories
of him
through the ages
a sporadic undertaking
turning into
a raging infestation
a smoldering look
constituting an
intense realization
that he will
always be
hooked

IN SHEEP'S CLOTHING

waiting for you
to make the first move
lips quivering in delight
as you wave goodbye
to a woman
who looks a fright
a tangled and messy up do
pouring sweat
as you prove
that she is worth more
than all those
previously removed
a firm handshake
withstanding each
and every demand
annoying questions
irking you
while answering
as best you can
an endorphin-filled high
replacing discrepancies
which will inevitably
slip and then slide
her sarcastic remark
and slanted eyes
staring at your
handsome face
in order to emphasize
what lies beneath
her pink and
blossoming sky
telltale signs
and a limitless belief
knowing full well
whom and what
she will believe

COVETED

catching the eye
of a worthless man
sizing you up
as you utter
a quick reprimand
an embarrassment
which lingers
upon your cheeks
a rosy blush perking up
within soft, cotton sheets
a disastrous unfolding
of events
making no sense
for you are both
pasted together
with the help
of a flourishing hand
caressing folds
of your skin
which remind him
of a double chin
belonging to his other woman
who yearns to be let in

SUBTLE PROSE

twirling long,
blonde braids
as a burst of
Florida sunshine
works its way
through your day
voices from the past
making themselves
at home to stay
for a mid-winter's
gathering
urging dancing
daffodils to sway
along with dandelions
curving their way
around delicate ankles
a belligerent crowd
of weeds
collecting themselves
in droves to weave
a pale, silent road
amongst brittle
branches and leaves
a mind-affirming rest
as you unfold
a lace hanky
and sneeze away
the past
monotonous days
growing noticeably
more bereft
for all that is left
is a lone, fragrant rose
gathering the strength
to recite a subtle prose

ANTIBODY ARMY

a quickening pulse
and a rapid heartbeat
throwing you off course
a quick intake of breath
acknowledging an
aching, painful sore
still lingering is
a contaminating virus
wreaking havoc upon
tiring veins
frigid icicles forming
crooked lines
administering to a
flailing pain
intuiting
an evasive ending
to all which has been
withstanding
a high fever
alleviated by
an all-natural,
home-remedied source
the relentless dawning
of sensitive, nerve endings
which respond with
a brutal force

HAVING YOUR SAY

take a moment to listen
for I will speak my peace
you are an uncaring being
interested in your own
selfish beliefs
dragging your feet
and shrugging
your shoulders
in utter defeat
while feigning interest
in her deep sigh
of relief
an insurmountable distress
adding up to figures
which have come out less
than what you are
willing to invest
striking a dubious pose
while being locked up
within that self-serving
mind of yours
because of you
she has grappled
and delayed
major life decisions
put on hold
as you continuously misbehave
a child existing
within the mind of a
forty-year old juvenile
acting out with
a solemn nod
and malevolent smile

SLIGHTLY SOUND

biting your nails
in angst and worry
as torn skin
and bloody cuticles
are ripped away
in a hurry
a raging fury
enveloping you
as a bitter argument
ensues
delicate ears
which are able to hear
a variety of distorted,
imagined fears
the tick-tock
of an ancient clock
mimicking your
pulse rate
and hands which begin to shake
a bipolar disorder
collapsing you
as you break
tumultuously working
its way through
as you surrender
and try to keep
your cool
taking into account
fragmented,
senseless words
which churn inside
your small girth
cursing the absence of
reasonable, logical signs
attributes which
have been overlooked
while constructing
a slightly sound mind

MOTH TO FLAME

oblivious to days which
grow considerably longer
sore muscles and a
dreary fatigue
wrapping itself around
broad shoulders
a summer sunrise
giving way to
chilly frostbite
as a long-legged beauty
wraps herself around
the mysteries of night
a flaxen-haired queen
laughingly displacing
your can of
shaving cream
harsh bristles
inhabiting her
round brush
encouraging you
to touch
her leftover stuff
clumps of hair
and powdery make-up
leaving smudges
and streaks
in your bathroom sink
short tendrils
peeking out
from around
luminous eyes
mischievous flecks
of gold and gray
making you distrust
your ability to survive

SLOW PENANCE

pulling you out
from under your feet
a fluffy, down comforter
forming a makeshift seat
your aching limbs
partaking in
a dangerous
tumble and spill
regrettably announcing
a premature ending
to an invigorating thrill
trailing after him
wrapped up in soft sheets
feather-light and silky
like sand on the beach
a subdued lamplight
casting shadows
upon tan cheeks
an exquisite form
deceiving you
as he removes himself
with a pent-up sigh
of relief
a churning stomach
unable to fully comprehend
a bed now made neat
requiring an Alka-Seltzer
to help calm
the torrid recollection
of a hapless rebound
a growing apprehension
and nervous strain
unfairly placed upon
your delicate frame
reluctantly coming
to the realization
that this was all
just a derisive game

LOCKING HORNS

resolving to put up a fight
within the throes
of a fiery, wintry night
unraveling, discourteous curls
standing straight up
in a fright
a tangled mess
initiating a manic
and impulsive dare
grabbing sharp scissors
in order to cut off your hair
oblivious to his indifference
for he will never care
about what
you have witnessed
placating compliments
getting you nowhere
as a deliberate denial
urges you to hide
behind a grim smile
remembering what
has been said
as he openly admires
a tawdry brunette
a rush of invaluable insight
erasing the full moon
which glows
an unattainable,
faraway light
furious waves
crashing upon
your shore
as you allow him
to walk away
and then call
an unanswered telephone
left to ring
in an otherwise
vacant hall

SMOOTH SAILING

downright offensive
are words
slipping past the
bruised, chapped lips
of an adolescent girl
trying to destroy his world
by exposing sordid secrets
better left untold
a short, cheerleader's skirt
riding up creamy, white thighs
a distracting surprise
forming tan lines
around his eyes
the eerie glow of
a miniature nightlight
casting dim and dull rays
upon a temporary respite
tears forming
squiggly, shadowy lines
continuously dripping
down her wooden blinds
unable to move
a single bone in her body
for she is sick of
his self-absorbed, pity party
scrunched up
into a self-contained ball
while thinking of a way
to apologize for it all
opening up her big mouth
after he has already
forgotten about
the various reasons why
he has had to pout

A SPIRITED ANTHEM

the trampling of feet
forcing you
to the edge
of your seat
a mud-splattered floor
littered with
sticky residue
you have come
to abhor
waiting for your
fellow enthusiasts
to sit down
and shut up
for you have had
enough of
juvenile behavior
littering with
Styrofoam cups
the spurt and fizz
of light beer
intoxicated men
who gawk at
beguiling cheerleaders
wearing pompous sneers
streamers and balloons
announcing relentless
adversaries
opponents who
bait and tackle
a momentous victory
cheering on
your favorite team

as you lean your elbows
upon your knees
taking a quick sip
of your drink
as you turn around
to confront those
who animatedly
shriek and scream

A SECOND LANGUAGE

impatiently tapping your foot
as a long sentence
of disturbing words
complain about
what they have heard
a persistent doubt
entering a rambling,
talkative mouth
a hesitation detaining you
from finding out
what he is all about
letters developing
a mind of their own
as you hear them
take on a sullen tone
a minor ailment
turning into
a raging infestation
of brutal words
forcing themselves
into his world
paragraph by paragraph
and a leaking, ink-filled pen
sabotaging poignant
memories of smooth,
summer skin
a sweltering heat emanating
from his darkening tan
as you fall blindly
into thickening quicksand
a burst of inspiration
knocking at your door
as you try to ignore
his rumbling snores
jotting down notes
in a hasty matter
requiring patience and aptitude
to ensure proper grammar

PUTTING ON AIRS

a lighted mirror
illuminating a haggard,
wrinkled face
artfully arranged
pigments and hues
affirmably
stating their case

shimmery glosses
and lipsticks
half-finished
accompanying
soft-bristled brushes
which relentlessly fidget

sneaking a peek
at a face requiring
a touch of make-up
to resume
impatiently waiting
for him to
change his tune

a cordial assessment
of what has gone wrong
a deep contemplation
yearning for
wrinkles to be gone

willfully erasing
the effects of aging
with a desperate prayer
almost worth saying

a silky-smooth,
age-defying cream
reassessed
as you deny the urge
to become obsessed

tweezers waiting
to pluck out fine hair
a chin held high
while putting on airs

WEARING THIN

bowled over by his
apparent lack
of interest
myriad reasons
alluding to
why he has
been indifferent
a reflection of you
hearing the words, "I-do"
a loveless union
confirming that
you are through

a hunk of a man
worthy of a thousand
reprimands
willing to fight
with an iron fist
and sword
by his side
an uninhabited fury
enveloping you
as you momentarily
start to cry

forced to think
on your feet
for you are
continuously bombarded
by angst and defeat
wishing to trade
it all in
for a scorching
rush of heat

experiencing a brush
with fate
as you try to gain
his attention
as of late
a luminous day
shining red-hot,
summer rays
making you sweat
with embarrassment
after having
been provoked
to misbehave

an incorrigible flirt
stepping out
in a tight, mini skirt
a gift-wrapped,
summer dream
proving to him
what you had
once believed
untying satin ribbons
of unconditional love
now demeaned

never knowing
what he is thinking
a man who stands out
despite your
stomach sinking
always gravitating
towards the magic
of him
a raging, incessant sin
wearing thin

RUN OF THE MILL

resisting the impulse
to ignore his
condescending thoughts
a sizzling summer
which should have
been spent at a
Caribbean resort

failing at
amicable conversation
for he has given birth
to a limitless amount
of work
packing your bags
and ripping off
old, luggage tags
as a silly thought
occurs

a wavering belief
dictating that
he is the one
you should keep
only to depart
all alone
a private destination
graciously welcoming
you home

catching you by surprise
is the inhabited
sanctuary of his eyes
encouraging you
to throw away
a torrid recollection
of all that you despise

ready to beg and plead
for a second chance
as you hold your breath
and then breathe
assuming that
a dire situation
has been addressed
just to have him leave

a heavy burden
placed upon your shoulders
as you leap at the chance
to grow even bolder
chasing after him
after you swore
that this relationship
was over

CHEMICAL CALLING

a mysterious stranger
gazing upon
your voluptuous figure
rows of organza and lace
framing your delicate,
luxurious cape
an exquisite gown entailing
dazzling, decadent jewels
the configuration of
a million stars
which shine upon
your flirtatious,
jovial mood
a natural inclination
to mingle and drink
for there is no time
left to think
glorious moments
when he sunk his teeth
into your skin
a slight trepidation
after reluctantly giving in
sharp fingernails
scratching and clawing
all for the sake of
a chemical calling
the untimely interference
of three, uncomfortable words
instigating an abrupt ending
to your safe
and sheltered world
blatantly ignoring
what you have heard
as you continue to
entice him with
just a single word

LOSING YOUR GRIP

losing your grip
as you
tumble and fall
cushioned by your
massive hips
as you start to
cry and brawl
an excruciating pain
which will take
a long time
to go away
wondering if you can
enlist the help
of a stranger
who is determinedly
walking your way
pushing yourself up
upon bruised elbows
for you are feeling
more conspicuous
than ever before
a scarlet, red embarrassment
heating up your
inflamed cheeks
fumbling to fix your skirt
while hoping
to appear meek
an unabashed feeling
coming over you
as you rush to become
the perfect jewel
sauntering along
a brick-paved sidewalk
as your static-clinging slip
peeks through

READER'S CHOICE

flipping through
a brand-new book
as uncreased,
smooth pages
beg you to look
momentarily distracted
as the sun blinks and sets
for all you want to do
is curl up
for a much-needed rest
a private exhibition
of colorful graphics
and pictures
enticing you to form
your own biased opinion
analyzing what
it all means
as the overwhelming usage
of rampant verbs
inhabit a vacant scenery
a controversial story
consuming you
as you endlessly compare
your mediocre life
to one which is
exciting and new
each turn of the page
initiating an intoxicating
turn of events
for you have always
secretly craved
an adverse, scintillating
circumstance
regrettably marking
your place
as long, drawn-out
sentences
refuse to behave

TUNNEL VISION

lucid memories
waiting to be plowed
along with
thick snow
accumulating
into raging doubt
precious time
set aside
to recuperate
braving harsh,
weather conditions
as you traverse
unknown terrain
ready to regain
proper footing
yearning for
bright, summer days
soon to be returning
a midwinter's thaw
leaving you breathless
and in awe
gazing at shooting stars
while wishing to grow
inordinately tall

A DECORATIVE MAINSTAY

a determined,
focused heart
manipulating
all which has tried
to tear you apart
a calm, melodious day
spent alongside
a desolate seashore
and a makeshift cave
sharp sunlight
and docile waves
introducing an illuminating,
decorative mainstay

bare feet
leaving imprints
in the sand
drawing stick figures
which resemble a
hunk of a man
a smug satisfaction
creasing your brow
as you chase after
a rainbow spectrum
heading south

an exquisite vision
hovering above
a vast array
of colorful bands
a darling perfection
separating the horizon
from the top of your van
an appealing figure
evolving into
sizzling sun
a sparkling manifestation
which would never
reveal itself
to just anyone

MORE THAN WILLING

an opportunity granted
to review your case
frustrating tears
trickling down your face
a deafening rattle
and a high-pitched sound
hands covering your ears
as you turn around
a slight touch on your shoulder
and a firm grip
forcing you to state
all that you are
willing to admit

attempting to forfeit
for you have always believed
that outright honesty
was the way to report it
messing with perfection
as you unload
unexplained discrepancies
in his direction
unable to calm down
after achieving the ability

to glare into his devious eyes
a blatant gesture
which would have intimidated
the most arrogant of guys
smooth skin serene
while making it
impossible to believe
that you are the only one
in whom he has
implanted his seed

a blank look
as he proceeds to
read his paperback book
spectacles laying
on your living room table
as you dare to look
a self-absorbed being
feigning a slight interest
in your meaning
after becoming aware
that you are
more than willing
to deceive him

A MOMENTOUS REJUVENATION

embellishing your
wrists and neck
with tiny mementos
which glitter and fold
a slight tremor felt
as you react
to shiny, brilliant gold
dainty chains
forming a slight crease
within a slim, rosy neck
a deep curvature of a spine
tingling after
what has been said

a foreseeable relationship
only if you haven't
been through it all
feeling as if
you will never
be in the mood for more
a fading inkling of desire
resuming its upright position
as you weigh
the pros and cons
of a delicate decision

LOVER'S LIFE PAST

time to assess
all which has occurred
in a Lover's Life Past
his smoldering look
and an interminable unrest
living in a state
of chronic sadness
and wavering disbelief
a crumbling foundation
coming together
to form one piece

leaving behind
a Lover's Life Past
so you can pretend
to start over again
searching for that
special someone
with whom you can trust
through thick and thin
and a frenzied, wild rush

thinking that you will be okay
as you gain
very little headway
a devastating hurt
buried in deep denial
for you still wish that
you can see him smile

knowing he will
never come back to you
yet fervently hoping
this isn't true
acknowledging the fact
that there is nothing more
you can do
for he will find someone else
with whom
he can make a fool

For D.